THE TEN COMMANDMENTS
FOR MODERN MAN

For Leslie

Am So ill...

[signature]

THE TEN COMMANDMENTS FOR MODERN MAN

Tad Flakowicz

Copyright © 2010 by Tad Flakowicz

All rights reserved. No part of this work covered by the copyrights hereon may be reproduced or used in any form or by any means – graphic, electronic or mechanical, including photocopying, recording, taping or information storage and retrieval systems – without the prior written permission of the publisher.

Library and Archives Canada
Cataloguing in Publication

CIP data on file with the
National Library and Archives

ISBN 978-1-926582-57-3

Tad Flakowicz
32 Killarney Court,
Brampton, Ontario, L6Z 3B6

This book is dedicated to the memory of my beloved daughter Yvonne who possessed an unusual paranormal talent that I never believed until a few years after her death when I heard her speaking to me. She spoke to me three times in a loud clear voice!

Yvonne existed like an Angel. It is no wonder that she achieved so much greatness so easily. She became the best GS Snowboard Racer in Ontario and was honored as the best young artist in city of Brampton Ontario, a city that dedicated to her memory one of its biggest Community Parks.

Think outside the dark box, think forward, backward, punch, kick left and right to come out of the box find the truth and come out of the darkness.

Do not fear the unknown, find a way to make it known!

Many thanks to Sarah Caloccia, my daughter's friend, who corrected my fluently broken English before publisher editing.

Front and back cover designed by Chris Arvai and Tad Flakowicz.

Content

Foreword	13
Introduction	25
Commandment 1: Loving God Above all Things	31
Chapter 1: This is a letter that should be read privately as it uncovers the deepest portion of a wounded soul.	39
Commandment 2: Do Not Use God's Name In Vain	49
Chapter 2: Becoming Friends with God	55
Commandment 3: Remember To Keep Holy Day Lord's Day	61
Commandment 4: Love	67
Commandment 5: You Shall Not Kill	75
Chapter 5: Philosophy of Killing	81
Commandment 6: Do Not Commit Adultery	91
Chapter 6: What Is Going On	97
Commandment 7: Do Not Steal	101
Commandment 8: Thou Shall Not Lie	109
Commandment 11: Life and Death	115
Chapter 11: Present Life and Death	133

Foreword

About your author, Tad Flakowicz:

I am told that I came in as a saviour! I was born in Poland in 1944, the last year of the Second World War in a one bedroom apartment. While a doctor was assisting my mother in my birth, Germans soldiers were clearing the apartment building, taking everyone to concentration camps. When they entered our apartment, I was in the process of being born. The soldiers saw a screaming women and the doctor, and they froze! In that fraction of second they changed from soldiers to humans: they dropped their hands from the machine pistols they had hanging on their chests and they tip toed backwards with embarrassment. My father and my grandfather also survived as they were hiding under the bed at that moment. So! Where is my bravery medal for saving my family by coming in to this beautiful world at that crucial moment?

I know of this event from my grandfather, a great

story teller who would tell me many stories of when he was in a Russian prison during the First War World.

Perhaps my first memory is of the shock I got when I was a one year old. As the Germans retreating from advancing Russians, the German army blew up a humongous bridge, just one kilometer from our building.

I was in a stroller, outside the building getting some fresh air and sun. I was being supervised through a ground level window when it happened… The explosion was so strong that it popped the windows in a ten kilometer radius. Shattered glass rained on and around me from the three floors of the building I was in front of. The stroller was in a foot of non-tempered glass shards. I remember familiar voices, but foggy faces (maybe through the glass?). I distinctly remember them shuffling through the glass, left and right; saying "Is he all right" again and again. Perhaps this being my first "Near Death" experience it was memorable in detail.

So that was not my time to die. Perhaps God was saving me so you'd get to read this book…

My first year of life was filled with many remarkable adventures. Being born during a war creates many more opportunities for such adventures than normal…

These events place in the historical city of Krakow. I have always been proud of my home city. It has a huge river, Vistula, which flows around the castle of Wawel.

When that river was frozen, my father would pull me on a sled across river to make a short cut to work and to bypass the Germans control gates. My father worked in a German-owned hotel through the war, a privileged place with fewer controls. In his hotel service role, my father became friendly with German limousine drivers, so... he used to exchange Polish Vodka for much needed canned German military food. Picture that the sled I'd travel with me to work was maximally filled with the tons of vodka under me. No wonder I am an alcoholic now!

That was survival. "No nationality, country or religion to die for" (you can sing if you know what that is...)

At one time, a Jewish family showed up down town. The penalty for trying to help Jewish people was execution, you and your entire family, right on the spot.

To avoid this, some people approached my father and asked him if it was possible to smuggle the Jewish family a cross frozen river to connect them with Polish partisans who could smuggle them South toward Yugoslavia and on to England.

My father knew that it would be a bullet in the head for entire our family if they were found out. He knew he could smuggle them across the frozen river, but the challenge was how to move them (walking, no cars yet...) through downtown?

Guess who helped? Germans limousine drivers! The got a beautiful rides in limousines!

OK! This cost a Lot of vodka, but they were similarly risking getting a bullet in their head as well if they were caught. Lots of heroism...

Once this road was establish it was used many times but they use underground tunnels between old buildings from middle centuries.

To shift to another way of speaking, humans build their "karma" one way or another...

Then, next: Wow! The War is over! But...we go over to communism, is that good or bad?

Rich people in western country (who control the media) hate communism, because communism nationalizes banks, takes that humongous money it gets divided equally. What a bad idea... Reminds me of another fellow who, two thousand years ago, tried to bring democracy to the world and he was not very popular on a beginning...

But there's more to be said on this: here are some positive and negative values of communism as it was, and why it collapsed:
a) Best education system in a world-'free'!
b) Good health system
c) Zero tolerance for narcotics and criminals...
d) Superior science support.
e) They tried to eliminate mistakes of religion that murdered and tortured entire nations. (An unfortunate mistake that they made: they should modifying religion but they never, never should remove God!
f) But...communist leaders became greedy imperialists, pressing the working class down
g) And they attempted, unsuccessfully to establish

the value of goods instead of leaving this to a free market exchange like the "Stock Market". They eliminated small businesses and left in the huge monopolies thereby eliminating competition and stagnating efficiency.

(Contrast this to the social democratic systems we have in Scandinavian countries, a balanced and humanitarian system which provides for market efficiencies while satisfying the rich and the working class at the same time.)

So, communism collapsed! Why? It was utopian system. Too good to be true. Why? Because humans are not perfect!

Communist leaders became so greedy that they became richer than even greedy leaders in the West! So eventually they became "One family "with the West.

They joined! Now we see everyone screwing the working class, West and East, from the Front and the Back!

Why not, there is no practical enforcement of penalties for the really big crimes!

But what happens if the working class is so screwed that there is no more money and work to go around for them? There has been an intensive exploitation of the poor of China and India to keep things going for a bit. But how can the rich still profit from the sale of cheap Asian products at high western prices if they remove jobs in west? Simple, they've closed their eyes and kept doing it! How long can this hold up? Till a GM, Chrysler and housing market collapse occurs! What next? Bring some jobs here (salaries of hungry people will necessarily be reduced here) and we start to produce for China! But, we can't make a car for twenty thousand here and sell it to Chinese for five thousand! That won't fly.

From another perspective, every ten thousand years or so humanity goes back to a jungle. Think of the Incas, Egypt, Atlanta, Noah's Ark, and now its "GM & Chrysler".

Back to your author!

In 1967 I tried to initiate a private "capitalist" business in Communist Poland.

I was the son of a hotel chain director, my mother was a chartered accountant, and I, with a strong entrepreneurial spirit, decided to try to become a farmer. Up to that time I was an electronics technician and in terms of farming experience I had never even watered a houseplant.

My wife was from a farming family. I took advantage of that connection and I signed a contract with an East German company to raise ducks. I was certain this would be lucrative; an egg becomes a duck in a mere six weeks!!! I'd never seen duck farming, but I could do math and I saw simply that my investment would increase 10x, 30x, even 100x in short order!

Per the contract, chicks arrived including some food for them.

It was a steal! A gold mine! So, using the land

of my mother-in-law and I started building a 100m long coop, from concrete blocks!

I only had a German motorcycle MZ to move the blocks from their source 40km away. Yes, you are not blind – a motorcycle. I built a trailer that I pulled behind the motorcycle and I hauled 15 concrete blocks per trip. I believe I calculated that I needed twenty thousand blocks; I could do a maximum of two trips a day…I drove even in winter on snow! Finally, a dump truck driver who'd seen this act could not watch anymore. He delivered my entire load for two cases of beer. That is how it works in a communist system: beer is traded for free trucks, free time, free gas…

So, the blocks arrive, but a creek prevents them from being dropped right where they're needed. For the next two weeks I was carrying 200 tons for 15Hr a day about 300 meters.

Net result: my health collapsed, not a big deal, just it left me with limited stamina. However, I've always been pretty sporty, so it wasn't going to kill me that easily.

So, my wife and I decided to go west to work at English translation where one hour of labour bought a hundred labor hours in the East!

Our plan was to become temporary wage slaves in the West, then come home as millionaires.

It was more incredible than we could have imagined: we first received welfare in Denmark it was equivalent to the income that we planned would come from the duck farm. We mentally collapsed!

All that hard work we'd done! And we could receive the same income with no work?! What a beautiful Danish system.

At this time there was a large Polish Jew community in an emigration hotel and they became our family. At Hanukah/Christmas we'd dance Jewish-Polish dances and the candles that burned we neither religion's lights, just an illumination of our celebration to be alive.

Jewish people always seem to have good information and they inform us about Canada as an emigration opportunity.

While we love nature my wife and I are more technically educated so we needed to find an income from industry.

So considering it, what better place is there than Canada? 99% unpopulated and impressively high tech?

So, we did it, we kissed the polar bear and we love it! From Indians to skiing, from canoeing to camping, and all in between!

Beauty, eh?…almost…My wife get a good position in TD Bank Visa, me Project Leader in the leading German company AEG Telefunken, we both bought a house, we were on top of the world…Almost…We had a super talented daughter, that had some paranormal connection that we ignored at the time, not realizing that she used this for her successes.

At the age fourteen she won a moguls ski competition, at fifteen she won first national prize for best snowboarding movie! At sixteen she was the Canadian Champion, just six months from Nagano Olympic.

And then, she started became involved in the fight against the drugs...Unfortunately, if you fight against drugs you meet the drug people...and they have a money and power!

They give her the ride of the life, trying to scare her. Didn't work. Finally, they killed her.

So, almost-perfect Canada, are the bears dangerous? No, the people are!

I was not prepared, my guard was down. I had no experience of drugs in my drug-free communist background.

My world collapsed! We were in our fifties; too old to have another child. I chose to sell everything and invest money in Mutual Funds, expecting security as I slowly awaited death. Again, coming from the communist system with zero tolerance for criminals, my guard was down. I trusted Canada. Then, a dishonest investment advisor stole all my money. My entire life savings plus the money I'd earned with my own hands across 40 years by building three cottages during the weekends. The RCMP and the Ontario Financial Commission spent six years trying to use a butterfly net to catch that fellow, but if I put his name here they'll arrest me in five minutes. What a beautifully crooked democracy. In communist Poland, he would have received an automatically death penalty. Perhaps you think this would be better? Don't forget that in communist society, you could receive the death penalty for what you merely said!..

So, let me tell you where this book really comes from...

I lost my biggest love, my joy for living, and I lost all the money that I accumulated through my years of very hard work...

I am living corpse. I thank God that I signed my house to my wife so I have a roof on a top of my head!

I spent twelve years studying to see if I can see my daughter again.

I studied religion and found absolutely no answers. Their doctrines are absolute, closed in a two thousand year old time capsule...

In parallel during that twelve years are run a charity "Flower power", using snowboarding and summer camping as sporty tools to recover children that lost family stability.

Where these come from? Two weeks after mine daughter die, biggest television network, TSN, call me that my daughter win a first price in national competition for best snowboarding movie. When I told them that she die they could not believed. I received in her name artistic hand carves snowboard that is hanging now in her room. Name of the movie was "Flower Power", referring to an artificial flower that was attached to her snowboard for a "good luck". As an artist she created spectacular title page that I used as a charity logo.

But real decision to create charity comes when

Italian musician group from Woodbridge Ontario, that my daughter skateboard with, recorded a song to her memory and distributed in music stores. They show up at my doorstep with thousands of dollars that I do not know what to do with it! So, I reveres situation, if I am parent that loss a child, must be a children that lost a parent. So I collected mentally depress children and I snowboard with them in a winter and travel on a canoe in a summer trough Canadian wilderness using a sport as untydepression tool. I accept also children from "healthy" but not sporty family and they donate a money to our charity "Yvonne's Camp's for Children".

I moved on to philosophy and analytic progression: being educated in electronics I tried logical analysis based on my direct experience.

For example:

If an electrical current flows from point "A" to a connection via a wire to point "B", I can measure both points with a meter and both measurements will be identical.

If the measurement at point "B" is zero I know that a wire is broken.

By extension, my experience has brought me to the following conclusions:

Near Death Experience - People can communicate from the afterlife.

Hypnosis indicates that there are previous lives.

In this life, we need to use our interpretation to choose meaning; Commandments would be powerful to guide our current experience.

Hence, this book is my best to provide a current version of that guide.

INTRODUCTION

We have many scientists, professors and religious people who write books about life, death, love, hate, life before birth and after death. But it is not education which creates feelings. You do not have to be educated to die!

When my daughter died they sent me too many psychologists and psychiatrists. I saw everything in black and white. I was ready to give my life to save goodness and to destroy any evil. These psychiatrists are like movie directors. They try to create artificial pictures from their books and try to imprint their pictures on me! These people write about, and read about swimming but they never get their feet wet.

I asked one of them "have you ever hit your thumb with a hammer when trying to drive a nail into a piece of wood?" He answered "NO, BUT I HAVE READ A LOT OF BOOKS ABOUT THAT." That is the difference between normal people and educated people who see things through a prism of books.

This does not mean that educated people are not normal, but is it possible that they could be?

Don't get me wrong, these educated people are logistic thinkers and they eliminate lot of "YES and NO" in an unknown world, and come to a conclusion.

They have even created a scale of death that measures the depth of being dead in a near death experience. And, why not? It's so simple. It is right in front of our eyes. Perhaps that is why we cannot see it; it's too close. It's the same as when Newton discovered gravity only after the apple fell on his head!

The most touching stories are the ones from people who have gone through some unusual spiritual process by themselves. Unfortunately there are not too many of them. Most of the authors of books on spiritual matter have Dr. or PHD attached to their names. Remember, the title of Dr and PHD will be stripped from their names by death like a coat of varnish from old furniture. They are like policeman or teachers, having a different face at work, but they come home and they cannot control their own children, spouses and lives. So, they did not get their feet wet....

What is so special about me that I have the right to write this book? I was touched by Angel! But I do not know if I have the guts to tell you about it! If I do, the next chapter will be "Vision". If it is not there that means I chickened out... or maybe it will be the chapter after that.

This book is looking for answers in a modern world. Too see and understand the image of God in a new light. People have hungriness for God and beliefs that are not satisfied by attending religious houses or explained by two thousand year old Doctrines.

For people in this century who have had Religion introduced to them by their parents it is not enough to hear two thousand year old stories about one fellow who walked on water and another who walked through water, and believe them.

People have become disconnected with the meaning behind the stories as they stand bored in their places of worship staring at the dandruff on the back of the person in front of them, or at the pretty girls sitting nearby (that's fun). They are not experiencing faith. They are hearing religion. So, you donate money to remove your guilt, or just to quiet your conscience to safeguard yourself, just in case something does exist out there...

This book is based on the Ten Commandments with new interpretation fitting to modern life.

Moses was a Messiah as was Jesus; there is no question about that. Jesus was spiritual teacher and was sent to suffer on earth. Moses was a Ruler sent to inform and create rules of discipline for human beings.

Both of them we can interpret today with much higher intelligence and understanding than the people two thousand years ago!

Moses was in a difficult position when the Israelites were in tough times and he asked God to bring rules of law and morality for the people of the times. The problem is that in today's times when you have a showers, television, wall to wall carpet and a car on your driveway, are these rules 100% applicable? The answer is simple and depends on the situation.

When you live in the desert you don't eat pork because it gets rotten very quickly and becomes poisonous. When you have a refrigerator to preserve things, pork on the barbecue is a most beautiful food! So too, kosher food was created for basic hygiene and over time became a beautiful tradition. But it is not necessary in the refrigerators age. In the Christian world Holy Sunday was observed but in the modern world it is obsolete when we work shifts, service or entertainment jobs, as long as we take one day a week off-we are Holy!

So these rules and traditions were created two thousand years ago not necessarily by God for Religious reasons but by educated Religious leaders who recognized that people needed to be protected from infectiousness disease. But it is not applicable today. So let's look Ten Commandments for today and give you a solid ground to stand on.

Let's first briefly analyze Moses' Ten Commandments.

We see that commandment number six is duplicated in commandment number nine as they are both referring to adultery in different ways. Similarly,

Commandment number seven and Commandment number ten both talk about possessing the goods of someone else. So, for practical reasons Commandments number nine and ten will be eliminated. But we are going to add Commandment # 11 that will be commandment called ''Life and Death''.

Being in the harsh desert and living in his difficult situation Moses forgot that he was alive! That he was born! He most importantly that he was going to die one day! He thought for his Nation were survive, survive, and survive. So his point of view was very much biased. He was occupied with the present and did not consider birth or death, or before and after life. He was in the present due to the difficulties of the situation. So let us go back to the basics and analyze where we are.

Come out of the dark box, think forward, backward, kick left and right to find the truth and expand it. If you stay quiet and you don't ask questions you are limiting yourself. Remember that people create Religion and they have absolutely no ability to punish you or put any curse on you for questioning things. All of God's messengers Moses, Jesus and Mohamed came outside of the human box and connected directly to Him. You can too.

Commandment 1
Loving God Above all Things

God is infinity. He does not have a line so he created a spiritual world as close to perfect infinity as was possible. He created the world that we have to come back many times to improve ourselves to get closer to perfection of infinity goodness. The more difficult life is the more we learn and the less we have to come back here. The combined goodness through our lives is "karma" so we have to listen to our hearts because the highest form of progression is acts of kindness; the good we did for other and not for ourselves.

One is born into a random universe, struggles for survival and pleasure and eventually dies. What is the point of living? There is no point. Why not die? Are you too afraid to die? So keep living! We are spiritual beings having physical experiences. We are all going to die sooner or later so why not practice for something that is going to happen anyway? So build that karma like soldiers build their skills in artificial battlefields. Karma is not fate for humans. It is Free will that creates ones destiny. It refers to the actions and reactions in our present and previous lives and determines our future.

In the midst of peace soldiers carry out manoeuvres against a nonexistent enemy. When it comes to reality they don't bend their heads down with the first whistling bullet. In our society we are not allowed to talk about or even think about own death. We should practice policy and deed so that fortune does not catch us unprepared for something that we must do at some time or another.

Imagine yourself standing in a back alley with a criminal pointing a gun at you. You will have so much less fear the more you practice. You will have less fear to run into a burning house to save people. You will not panic during a car accident and you will control the car as long as possible. And last but not least you will lessen your fears against your boss...

To create your faith you must clean house and deal with your fear of death. And now, we come to the most fundamental question of human kind:

a) Are the people who go to churches, synagogues, mosques or other religious houses, are they disbelievers who are scared of death looking to someone to reassure them?
b) Or are they believers who have repeated someone else's prayers to the point that they have become believers to their own brainwashed conscience?
c) Remember, "A lie repeated a thousand times becomes truth" Humanity is based entirely on that the same as politics and religion.
d) Or do we start talking to our conscience creating our own prayers and communicate with God di-

rectly?

One must really step outside the box because praying someone else's prayers, singing aloud, bowing your head in front of a plastic figurine, watching women's dressing fashion, beautiful girls or looking at the dandruff on the back of the person in front of you is not faith. Remember, religion is not believing. It is a human creation that deviated according to geographical location to practice goodness so we can become believers. All disbelievers in Holy houses sacrifice animals (or even humans), sing, pray, put money into the collection plate and they are still disbelievers and scared of death.

So, how can they become believers? First they must step outside the box. This doesn't mean that you quit your Religion, no! Keep your religion as your part of your core and backbone. How can you do that? Very simple. Before we go to spiritual life let us analyze basic life on earth. What are the basic most important things in life?

a) Health
b) Love
c) Money

Let us start in reverse order:

A) Money
We go to church (or equivalent) and we pray O God! Give us money. Let me win the lottery.

Hmmmm.......That has been tried already and it doesn't work. Or fall onto your
knees and talk to your conscience. God help!

You go to the unemployment office and you read a job advertisement in the paper, talk to friends who have a business looking for work, and put an advertisement in the paper or into a Church bulletin. Ask the Priest to ask people to list house renovations in Church for unemployed contractors who belong to the Parish. Let the Priest sweat a little because God prefers sweating over singing. And now, go and make money.

Now come to your empty religious house made of cold concrete. Make it Holy and warm it up with your prayers.

God thank-You for the money. And, you find the first light of your soul. God makes you create prayers from your hearts, not to repeat someone else's words.

B) Love

There are many kinds of love. Love for a child, wife or stranger. You can stop in the nearest flower shop and buy flowers for your wife, buy a toy for a child, go to a religious house and pray and thank God for love. Give a child a toy and flowers to your wife. It is simple. It is inside of you. Do not be shy. Toys and flowers are the key to opening your soul. To love yourself is not easy. When I am approached by the homeless and asked for a quarter I answer "go to work!"

A few years later I was touched by an Angel. I met him again and I gave him $10 likely for 6 beers and I watched him dance away. Then I went and bought six beers for myself and do you know how much better that beer tasted? Does that mean that God is in the beer store too?

C) Health

Health and happiness go together. You are part of God and loving yourself means loving part of God. The primary of unhappiness is never in you, it is in your thoughts. Never say I am unhappy! Say "there is unhappiness in me". The cause of unhappiness is never a particular situation but your thoughts about it. Separate your thoughts from the situation. The situation is always neutral. You are not! The situation is fact and you are thoughts. The thoughts are involuntary automatic repetitiveness. Strictly speaking, if you are free skating through this world then you don't think. Thinking happens for you. All bodily functions happen for you. Your conscience, your coach, your guardian Angel, your spiritual task that you came here to fulfil is working for you so you are at the mercy of the voice. Digestion happens, circulation happens, thinking happens. The voice in your head has a life of its own. Most people are at the mercy of the voice but if you have strong enough will you can build your karma much faster by doing more good things for others. Take your human power and show your coach or guardian Angel that you are doing more goodness than you were assigned spiritually from above. But if you become too spiritual you can become obsessed and blind and do not only good, but also killing stealing and politically enslaving an entire country, in a name of spirituality! If you become too physical you can become a killer, a rapist or even worse; a dishonest politician. The only mercy for you is to stop and take a big breath and think I am who I am, I can do well. I don't hate people around me. I am who I am. I build my karma. You run your body together with your intelligence, your conscience, your coach, or your guardian Angel. That is happiness; to create happiness for others. Love to be loved.

CHAPTER 1

This is a letter that should be read privately as it uncovers the deepest portion of a wounded soul.

In this busy life we do not realize that life is just a flash in a universe. We concentrate on the small shiny details like cars, extravagant houses, clothing and jewelry, losing the general picture and not having our feet on the ground.

As the great philosopher Seneca said; "Some men have shrank so far into dark corners that objects in bright daylight seem quite blurred to them." Meaning that people cannot differentiate right from wrong, or victims from attackers as they are looking only at outside appearance; the shiny surface.

Three questions to consider are: Who we were before we were born? Who we are now? Who we will be after we die?

A) Who are we now?

Due to the eating process our entire body (all flesh and bones) are replaced in a less than one year. We become a completely new person physically. So, why can it be that you are the same person if you have changed 100% physically?

This is because people exist on two levels one being physical and one spiritual. These two components of the same body will be referred to as the "physical you" and the "spiritual you".

It is interesting why when we change entire physical body, our passport or driving license are the same? Maybe these documents are spiritual as well?!....Ha! Ha! Let get series.

B) Who are we before?

Where was "spiritual you" before your physical birth? It is a well known fact that through hypnosis it is possible to transport "spiritual you" back in time for a few days. Witnesses of the subjects recent past can verify that the memories and experiences uncovered through hypnosis were true thus proving that hypnosis is truth. What if we transport "spiritual you" back ten or twenty years before birth? You are able to talk about details of your life that occurred ten or twenty years before "physical you" was even born. The hypnosis process doesn't change. We have to believe that the "spiritual you" is telling the truth regarding the experiences occurring in the period before physical birth in the same way that we believe the "spiritual you" told the truth in few days of hypnosis.

C) Who are we after?

We have to reference people who have had Near Death Experiences (NDE). Many cases of NDE have been reported after an individual has been pronounced clinically dead and has come back to life again.

Scientists and theologizes are afraid to discuss

this subject as both are afraid of losing the credibility of their education and knowledge and of losing their reputation as there is not enough tangible scientific evidence explain this phenomenon. Scientists and Theologizes would have to admit their limited ability to explain this phenomenon and how little they truly know about the subject. They would lose their "guru" reputation.

Let us collect information from the experiences of many people who claim to have and a Near Death Experience (NDE) and divide them into three categories based on length of time "dead".

A) The first category is Death for a few minutes. In this case the subject reports that they saw their body from above but they had no spiritual experience.
B) The second category is Death for longer period. In this case the subject reports having a spiritual experience.
C) The third category is Death for much longer time. In this case the subject reports having multiple spiritual experiences during their period of death.

Let's put aside the medical details surrounding the subjects NDE and analyze the spiritual experiences reported by the subject. To analyze the three points above, we go to researchers who construct Weighted Experience Index in order to measure the depth of NDE on a scale. I will simply call this the

"Scale of Death"

In point A there is clinical death and doctors officially pronounce death due to no vital signs, cardiac arrest and lack of brain function for a longer time than medically permitted where no reversible biological action is possible. We cannot explain how. Perhaps some part of the brain has died and maybe another part of brain took over resulting in this miraculous recovery and the patient suddenly wakes up.

We can adopt the explanation that the situation is simply not explainable at the time and try to match a theory back to the situation in an attempt to explain what happened after the fact. This is similar to how a mechanic has to change half of the parts in your car one by one ruling things out to finally be able to explain what the initial problem was.

Even scientist like Bruce Greyson and Michael Sabom challenge the belief that consciousness can function independently of brain activity.

The Lazarus Phenomenon is the spontaneous return to of blood circulation after resuscitation has failed. This Phenomenon gets its name from the Biblical story of Lazarus who was raised from the dead by Jesus.

But, that was two thousand years ago and maybe the story became twisted. Let's consider modern cases. You can go on the internet and search hundreds of reported cases of NDE, but I choose this one. This experience talks about the idea of "tasks to be completed" in life before you can die and move on.

In 1982 a woman in Australia left her work and had a car accident on her way home. She was pronounced dead by and experienced doctor of neurosurgery and transferred to the morgue.

A long enough time had passed that doctors were able to locate her parents and they were able to arrive at hospital. On their arrival doctors inform them about her death explaining that she had no chance of survival due to the severity of her injuries.

Suddenly a young nurse burst to the office screaming "she is alive". She sat up and said "Don't give me any more drugs!" The patient then fell into a deep coma for ten days.

Now that was our world and what people in the hospital saw that day. Let's see what the patient's "spiritual self" experienced at this same time and see what she says about where she was during the time period that she was clinically dead.

Here is what she said; "I was traveling very fast, headfirst through the dark of what looked like black boiling clouds, ahead was a tiny dot of bright light steadily growing and brightening as I drew nearer. I arrived in an explosion of glorious light into a room with insubstantial walls, standing before a man in his thirties. He welcomed me with great love, tranquility and peace-no words. He directed me to look to my left, where my life was replaying .I relived those moments and I felt not only what I had done but also the hurt I had caused. Some of the things I would have never imagined could have caused pain.

I was led further into the room. They're coming towards me was my grandfather .We hugged. He told me that grandma was coming soon to join him. He told me she had a cancer. When I came back to life and told my mother, she got very angry at me. How can I know months before she was diagnosed?

The person who first welcome me came and placed his hand on my shoulder and turned me toward him. He said;"YOU MUST RETURN.YOU HAVE TASK TO PERFORM" Tough! He never mentioned what my task was!

What was her task? Is her task to live with the pain that she received as a result of the accident for many years? Is she supposed to serve a better purpose and do good things for other people before she departs? At least she received the wake up call to learn that there is something on the other side.

What about me? Do I have a task and what is it. Why am I still here? What task have I not completed yet? My seventeen year old daughter was brutally killed! My best love, my best companion, my soul, my life and my reason to live!

What about all of you? Why do you not know what your tasks are?

Why? Is earth a place we come to suffer for the sins of a previous life? Let me know, because I don't know if I should love or hate!

God! Where are you?

Let's go back to a drawing board and start the next chapter.

Read this book slowly, one chapter at the time. Then re-read it and sleep on it or else you may choke yourself by eating too fast.

COMMANDMENT 2

DO NOT USE GOD'S NAME IN VAIN

Commandment number 2 is not to use God's name unnecessarily. Should we be scared of God? Is He good or bad? Is He like a baseball bat hanging on top of us, ready to hit us any time? Or, is He loving, allowing us free will and trying to help us to correct our mistakes? Or, is He allowing us to live decent and moral lives by injecting into our consciences and speaking to us continuously? Consciousness is what makes us to do things right or wrong and when we do

wrong we have a sense of guilt. That is what stops us from jumping out of airplanes without a parachute or grabbing the blade of a knife (unless we're mentally sick, politically or religiously brainwashed-which is not too different).

It is possible that the same conscience drives our hearts, lungs and our vital organs. So, if "someone" continuously talks to us, can we talk back? Yes! We are continuously asking ourselves questions such as should I do this or should I do that? And a scale inside of us always leans to one side unless it is equal 50/50.

But can we in this modern era ask very strong controversial question? Does God have the Internet? The answer is surprisingly- yes! God has the Internet and you are the screen! And your fingers are the keyboard. You are typing your own life!

The sun's rays touch the earth to warm it but the source of heat is far away. Our soul is similar. It possesses great warmth but it is sent far away from the source to posses new knowledge of greatness… .or not.

No one should feel pride of any thing that is not his own! No money, titles, houses or land! No size, intelligence, skin colour, nationality, health or disabilities. Everything was given to us, and will be stripped away with death like layers of varnish from old furniture. We will be left as naked as we

were born. The only thing we can take with us is the same amount of goodness we gave to others which is measured by the memories of the ones that we leave behind.

Maybe that is the task that we come here for and it is inside of us. This is why we can not see it. We're looking very hard all around us but it is so close that we can't focus on it .Your conscious speaks back to you all the time. If you are down and you are feeling blue take your conscious for a walk in the park at the nearest hospital, look up at the windows and say a prayer for whoever might be lying inside; that they may get well soon. They need more than you do! Because you are outside of the hospital!

Now, ask yourself what is your problem? Face it, first with your conscience and then analyze it, and face these same problems again. Even if you solve them partially (or avoid them if they're negative forces), it is worth it to say the Prayer "Thank You God" because the only Prayers that work are the Prayers that are completed physically before you start Praying.

Listen and talk to your subconscious, breath in deeply, one, let it go, breath again, no-one needs to know you're just breathing. Keep counting your breathing; this is your secret meditation. This is your secret religion, much for your level of intelligence. You are talking to your conscience. You are talking directly to God. You do not need to repeat someone else's words! We have too much intelligence and education is killing any religious or political beliefs. Everything our parents taught us about religion became with education, unbelievable like a children's story. But we are scared to admit this because we feel that there may be a power above us through our subconscious and we are as scared of death as people were thousands of years ago! Except, we don't have the comfort of religion anymore. So, we try to block any thoughts about the existence of God or death and push them away for later. But, later is now. We can die at birth or at a hundred years old. So, we don't have to be scared to step outside our religious box. No lightening is going to strike us! Because religion was created by humans to worship a God. That is why each geographical location has different religion, and people did not have a cars or television to exchange information and we do. That is why we have to step outside the box and adjust new thoughts, new prayers to a new situation in the present, past and future. I know! I know! God could have created cars or televisions long time ago, but He did not! He did not create the wheel either-humans did! He is our professor. He gives us the intelligence to be able to do these things like any professor does. He is proud when His students progress and even surpass Him with new inventions. THAT IS GOD'S ENJOYMENT OF HIS INVENTION—HUMANS!

Pay attention to Chapter Two. My seventeen year-old daughter brought a new invention to Jesus. The best state of mind is when we realize what our purpose is when we are born and we fulfill that purpose accordance to our own nature. Why these gifts that we receive are not shared equally we going to discuss in the next chapters.

Chapter 2

Becoming Friends with God...

The relationship between us and a God had lot of similarity to relationship between student and professor. Sometimes very talented students, here on earth, inhance knowledge obtained from professor, and when they departure they present new invention to God.

Imagine, Jesus sitting on his chair, and listening to a new invention, presented by his student. He will be smiling, praud of his student.

Is God mad about that? Definitely not! As any prophessor is proud about their students when he inject his knowledge into a student and as a seed it bloom into new flower of progression, is a success of the prophessor extended knowledge.

One of the examples will be invention of the wheel! God forget to create a wheel, we invent a wheel!

If God will create a wheel, you will see elephant or rabbit on wheels, but you cannot! And wheel invention was so significant that when was presented to Jesus, He has a smile of admiration for his student; He was prouder and happy of his investment into a student that bloom into a new invention!

When mine seventeen years doughtier die, she was Canadian Champion in Alpine Snowboarding.

She was born at 25 of December (at Jesus birthday), many people are born at this date, but me skeptical and technical person did not want to hear what other people were telling me, that she is special and she do unusual thinks, till we enter (firs time) room with eighty ski instructors, and during a meeting she whisper to my ear, telling me who is good pearson and who are a nasty characters! I ask here: how do you know, you never see them! She answers; dady I told you I can see a thinks that other people cannot see it. I remember I get goose bumps on entire body. I sow hers success in whatever she touch, but I pretended that I cannot see it, because I toad if I tale her how good she is doing, she will stop doing, so I hide my proud smile and I pretended I cannot see it. I toad it was a hard work combine with talent, but in any direction? I just did not turn a head any more to pretend that I cannot see it, because I toad that was a fluke.

Just before she dies, she says to me; "I finally figure it out!" I ask her, what did you figure it out?

She say;" I figure it out what is a haven and hell!" I ask what you mind.

She say; "Haven is up there, but hell is down here on earth; where we have a wars, killing, floods, earth quick, sicknesses and poverty. And we keep coming here till we became clear"

She was reporting that sometimes at night people in long dresses coming to her bedroom and telling her that she is "clear" and she can live any time... Maybe that why she die so young?

Above theory much perfectly Michael Newton theory, in his book "Journey of Souls", results that he obtained trough hypnotization of people and backing them before their birthday.

Only one was obtained trough pure scientific, other pure spiritual. What the much!

The strange think that she control 100% of crowd around her and she was not a forward pearson, she usually sit quietly in a corner, she put gently seed of friendship in yours hart, and she watered with her smile, till it bloom as a flower of friendship trough your head and you cannot resist her power.

Teacher, in a school, catch a small little poem that she past to her friend describing what is snowboarding;

> Is like being on a water,
> But truly through the clouds
> Is like of the ground, but grounded.
>
> Yvonne

So, after she became Canadian Champion and die just before Olympic in Nagano, can we ask her to become our representative, to present new device "snowboard" to Jesus? I think so...

So possible when you see lighting on a sky, is Yvonne zigzagging on a snowboard together with Jesus, on a perfect powder made of clouds.

Do you believe in angels? There are propobly souls who are "clear" just coming to help us in our difficult journey on earth, just using theirs smile.

PS ; So, what You think I have enough to share with you to pool out of the old myths ,and do not reject them just expand them , so you can think outside the box , expanding before and after! But wait, is more!

When she teach girlfriend snowboarding, yes,girl was a skier, but first time on a snowboard, she took her to a steepest slop, girl say; I do not want to die, Yvonne say ;why not? "Dyeing is most beautiful thing, there are unusual flowers and beauty on other side, do not be afraid!" Now we not taking about mental pearson, we taking about best student, best artist, best photographer, national champion, who control people in national level in adult division!

But last, but not the least that inspires me to write this book, me, technical, and analog disbeliever was Yvonne talking to me in a laude voice, one year after she die, laude like in football station speakers! She said:

"Daddy don't do it! Daddy don't do it! Daddy don't do it!" Directly into a braine!

Scary! But I cannot reject! I will talk to you abaut in a next chapters.....

I realize that my philosophical doctrines maybe disturbing to some, specially conservative people.

But at least I feel brave and feeling alive by receive pain of criticism, not as caution person, who do not express any opinion, playing safe and do not achieve any results so by not receive any pain, they feel dead being alive....

Commandment 3

Remember To Keep Holy Day
Lord's Day

Spoken in English this means don't work a seven day week. It is a sin if you work on Sunday. You don't bring money to church! They can not control you politically to tell you what to do!

But in a practical way it is simple. You are too tired to perform for seven days! So, you take one day off to rest.

If we work seven days we are too tired and our efficiency goes down. We need a rest. Fine, if we work for seven days we are too tired but who said the day of rest has to be Sunday?

The seventh day is a resting day. If we work a seven day week we have much less efficiency in the following days. That also applied to slaves a thousand years ago. So it is not for Holy reasons and it is not for mercy. It is business for slaves and is rules for rest of the people. JESUS was a superior philosopher. Let us see how the rest of the people twist this into politics and money. It is simple. You work for six days, and then you rest, with money! Let's create a religion and tax laws to take your money away!!! You come to any house of Religious Worship, for example, church, synagogue, mosque, Indian tent or cave and Religious ceremony tells you IN THE NAME OF THE GOD TO RE-

LIEVE YOUR SINS DONATE A MAXIMUM OF YOUR MONEY TO GOD, OR ELSE YOU MAY BURN IN HELL! And of course since clerical businesses do not pay taxes it must return the favour to the government and announce that you will burn in hell as well if you do not pay your taxes.

The same agreement was made between priest and Kings to kill other nations. Priests announce that is no sin to kill another nation because they do not believe in "our God" which translates into "they don't give money into "our God's pocket". So they kill them and divide goods between the Priests and the King! How do they turn disbeliever to believers? Ha! That is the beauty of religion; kill, torture and burn them! But, we discuss that in commandment #5. DO NOT KILL!

And it is no different between governments and churches only the government puts a policeman with a gun in the middle of the street and shoots you between the eyes if you don't give them any money! Legal robbery in the middle of the street that rich people call the ''law''. They call this taxes! What happens if they increase taxes to 100%? Lets discuss that in Commandment: DO NOT STEAL.

Let's see how many people work on Sunday.

Priest! Working hard for money! On Sunday!

I work in a television studio, to entertain rest of the people even on Christmas.

I work as a ski and snowboard instructor, especially on Holy Days.

Hospital and ambulance workers, weekend salesmen, contractors in emergencies, fire workers and thousands of people that provide a variety of services.

Who cares which day you take off, as long as you take off a day to rest...so simple right? WRONG! IF YOU DONT COME TO CHURCH ON SUNDAY WE CAN NOTCOLLECT YOUR MONEY!!!!!!!!!!!!!!!! HA! Is that God's idea, or have people created a political system to make a money and control people? Religious people did a lot of good by being more educated and controlling the misbehaviour of the general public thousands years ago. They created circumcision in a hot climate when people did not have a showers to keep themselves clean, or for hygienic reasons. They prohibited people from eating pork because they had no refrigerators. They prohibited Europeans from eating meat on Fridays because they hunted and ate too much meat. They scare Egyptian with sun-clip!

But these days are over. We work in television, ambulances, fire trucks, and we take a day off when we can. Ignore the old fashion idea of Sundays off as long as you take one day off!

Rest, who cares what day of the week it is. Old traditional fashion does not bring us spiritual values any more. They bring wars. They join with politics, power, killing and distraction they are one hundred percent money and power oriented. How can we celebrate a day off when so much is wrong?

Imagine there is no country or religion to die for.

Who sang that? Let it meditate……imagine. Imagination is a powerful tool. It is a form of meditation and also a form of prayer. Imagination creates energy around us and influences other energy and creates physical results. Remember to be careful what you wish for because there is no way back once it is completed.

It doesn't happen right away, or always. Most power full imagination happens when you are almost ready to fall asleep and you think "oh, if this happened!!!" Scary, but it will be completed in less than ten years!!! Why? It is simple. We have our conscience, our spiritual guides, and our pre-existing tasks that we come here to perform. Small suggestions from our guides at our weakest moments when we are almost unconscious and falling asleep directs us to the tasks that we are put here to perform. And once you are confused and you do not know if you pray, wish or do it, it has happened! That is strong direction from your subconscious guiding you to perform your task. The ideal state is when we realized that we have fulfilled the purpose that we were born for and we live in accordance with nature. Remember, you were not born for one particular corner of this world but the whole world.

Commandment 4

Love

Love your neighbor, honor your father and mother. These are basic concepts, but love is not something we can touch or see. Let's analyze what love is. Just as Raymond Moody developed scale of degrees of death, let's develop a scale of the different degrees of love.

What kind of love can a human being experience?

1. Love between Husband and Wife (only love when sex occurs)
2. Love for a Child.
3. Love for a Parent
4. Love for Brothers or Sisters
5. Love for Grandparents.
6. Love for Relatives.
7. Love for Friends.

Let's analyze the scale of the degrees of love in reverse, meaning from least to most strong. Specifically in the situation of grief after the loss of a loved one.

1. If we lose a friend we go to the funeral, we discus with other friends or relatives, and often

wonder how it is possible that someone so young could be taken away. Where is justice and where is God? We return home and call a few friends who miss the funeral and the next day we go back to work. Before we know it life is busy again and everything disappears. Life goes on!

2. Love for relatives will be a little stronger depending on how often they visit us and how much time is spent together. With every family event there will be memories and stories of this person. "Oh! Remember when Uncle Frank fell in the lake on our fishing trip and we had to dry out in a front of the fire place?" This is love talking, recorded and memorized in family members. There is more suffering here because family is missing that person in action. There is mourning and sorrow and a feeling of suction within the heart which represents a deeper degree of love.

3. The loss of a grandparent is very sad, but on the scale of death it is most expected. Mourning and recovery time is reasonable and will depend how close they were in a last few years. Love stay with us and we never forget them.

4. Love for a parents is stronger. To measure everything with the same ruler let's assume death occurs at old age and of natural causes. We remember the toys they bought for us and play-

ing with them/ We even remember the punishments that we receive as "smart, revolutionary teenagers".

We understand these punishments now as love. When parents are here with you, you always worry that you are going to lose them. When there are gone you have a feeling that there are with you still.

You can talk to them now more easily than before; you just close your eyes and talk to them. It's funny how easy it is to talk to them now when they are gone, and come to the realization that we lost so much valuable time while they were alive. Losing them is painful and leaves a scar forever. Mourning is longer, although it gets easier with the passing of time. Life still goes on and love stays with us forever.

5. The death of a brother or sister takes you by surprise. You cannot believe it. It is so shocking that you cannot fully believe it has happened until you see an open coffin in Funeral Home. The amount of grief deepens how close you were. Some siblings are glued together, others are not, nevertheless it takes a chunk of our your heart forever. This mourning never ends. It gets easier with time but you carry that love as a small log on your shoulders for life.

6. The love between a husband and wife is an institution. It consists of friendship and is multi-

plied by sex. Love for children, providing economical support from buying a fridge and keeping it full, changing the shingles on the roof, to making sandwiches for school. Losing one is like losing a supportive pillar under a bridge. You may not have even noticed that you were one with each other, and you have lost half of yourself. You have lost your daily support for problems at your work, your caregiver for your headaches and colds, and your sexual and financial partner. This is also your partner that did half of the work with the children. You are standing now in front of a ladder with no footsteps and with one leg cut off. And, life asks you to climb. You come back from the funeral and your children are sitting a front of you so you cannot even start mourning because you still cannot believe it happened. It helps to have the support of friends and relative to begin a new daily routine. Of course we have the tendency to reach for the one and only best antidepressant-alcohol. It is good, nothing to be ashamed of. Unfortunately this only works for one day and it make things much worse for following days after. If you have children you are lucky. In the beginning you don't see them, you don't see your responsibilities and everything seems worthless. HELLO! If you concentrate you can hear your subconscious talking to you and communication with you. You are half spiritual and you can hear your spouse talking to you through your subconscious. Yes you can! Ask yourself what to do and you can hear your spouse telling you what kind of sandwiches to make for the children to take to school. It will tell you to look on the side of the fridge for the hockey or figure skating schedules. YES YOU CAN TALK! Remember when you came home from work first (when yours partner was alive) you would ask yourself out loud "where did she put the figure skates? Where did she put those hockey skates? And, then the answer comes to you! You were not talking to yourself but through your subconscious to her and she guided you to find what you were looking for. YOU CAN DO THIS NOW! There is no reason to not talk to someone just because she steps to another room. And that's the LOVE.

7. What number is that? Seven? I am scared to start this one. It is the strongest love under the sun. It is the biggest love that God created and it is most painful. After my daughter died I could not find God! I stood in the middle of the Cemetery at 2 o'clock in the morning asking for any God or even a ghost to show up! Nothing! How evil is God that he can hurt somebody like that? I swear at God and told Him that one day He will have to answer me that—face to face and apologize for this cruelty and mistake. The next Sunday I went to church and the Priest just read "Thank God for the love and mercy that He

sends upon us!" Now, that is a good one. Just apply that one to me! I swore heavily and walked out angrily! Today I realize that swearing on God's name is the strongest prayer that human being can pray! Because if deep down if I did not believe that God existed then I would not be able to swear on His name. That was direct contact with God! Or, was I brainwash by my Catholic religion like anybody else in their own religions? I became like an animal in a cage. I thought that the only way out was through the death. I lost my religion. So I started reading philosophy in an attempt to find myself. That is the strongest love. So you have your scale of love!

P.S. It is a question if Jesus, suffering on a cross, did not want to show us direct relation between love and pain. As all who love Him, suffer accordingly to the amount of love that they posses for Him.

COMMANDMENT 5

YOU SHALL NOT KILL

Is killing right or wrong? Such a silly question. Almost stupid, isn't it? God tells you "do not kill" but at the same time God tells you to protect your body from harm including harming yourself (with a knife, gun, narcotics or alcohol). So, it is even more important for you to defend your body from being killed by the killer!

It is yours duty and it is your sin if you do not do it! God created you and only God can take you away! No policeman or soldier has the right to kill! But, you do have the right to kill a killer before he kills you. Even God fought Satan. Let's find out what our relation with God is in that matter.

God is infinity, the line between physical and spiritual life is constantly changing and we have consciousness from God and our own free will. We combine them and make right decisions which changes the shape of that line and influences not only our physical life but also our spiritual life, and builds our "karma".

But what about a situation when the killer kills your family but he doesn't threaten you?

Wow! According to the New Testament if somebody throws a stone at you, you should to throw bread at him. That is the New Testament that Jesus brought to us and all democracy is base on that. So explain to me why we can not explain to a big fish in a lake to not eat a small fish any more? Why does a wolf kill a deer? Why do bigger animals kill smaller ones? Why do stronger people kill (legally) weaker people or an entire nation? If Jesus brought us a new democratic testament why did He change this only on a paper? Why not in reality!? Why do I have to kill beautifully "Bambi" to eat? Why does God make us kill!? Wow! I don't know.

BUT GO AND KILL THE BASTARD THAT KILLED YOUR FAMILLY! Because of our law is based on New Testament only for the blue collared worker, and the Old Testament for the rich and famous. So, try to be as good as possible but use the Old Testament! Tooth for a tooth, and eye for an eye!

The pedophile who killed five times, and was released five times for good behaviour (or fully cured by "doctors") is freed and killing your child on his first day of freedom. That could not happen in a place that operates under the Old Testament because the parent of first child would have killed the bastard and the four other children would still be alive. The problem is that our law is like the parents of fighting children- they not interested who is guilty; they are interested in peace and quiet and punish both of them! Our law is similar. They rather lock up a noisy victim who is a difficult and embarrasses the police than look for the dangerous criminal. Let it

attack that noisy parent complaining about his child being raped and killed than the killer!

O YES! BY ALL MEANS! PUT THAT PARENT IN JAIL! MAKE IT QUIET! And it is much less dangerous for law enforcement and they can even beat him or kill, after all he is not violent so he is not dangerous! And how much pleasure is to do it?

Guns, teasers, Vancouver, Stalin, Hitler. And, that is our sick democratic society. So is killing according to a circumstance right or wrong?

You tell me! In my opinion killing a killer is morally right but our society criminalizes that action so therefore our criminal system has become morally wrong!

However if you don't kill a killer right away killing him later could be interfering with God's purpose for that individual.

So, how much time do you morally have to kill a killer of your family?

I would say, one year when you are still under emotional stress and after that leave it to God because it has became part of that purpose that God has for that individual.

And, after that time it becomes a question if you have not became a killer. Of course this is the general law meaning and it will depend on the individual situation and your guardian councilmen will coach through your conscience according to a moral law not a "democratic one.

PS. Training yourself as a killer is an only democratic system that can achieve a justice, only fist in a face can achieve a justice, nothing else can do it....

Chapter 5
Philosophy of Killing

Does this mean that there is nothing wrong with killing? Yes and not! Remember God was fighting Satan and evil forces. And He killed them! Or at least He tried! So, we kill evil too. At least in self defense...

Sooner or later we will die also. God designed us to die, so He also designed us to be killed. Does this mean that he is killing us? Maybe for Him, killing us is a form of transforming us from one life to another. For people who are unsure that life after death exists, all we know is that we will be dead. Hello? Did he make a booboo to not inform us of what is happening? We are scared. How are we going to call Him on this action? Is he transforming us, or simply killing us? Are we transformed or are we dead? If we know before we die that we are only transforming then we don't truly die. But, if we do not know that we are transforming then we do die.

Oh yes. How simple the truth is to analyze. So God creates not only birth but also death. But when is killing Holy and acceptable and when is it not?

Why can I not kill a killer of my family? Am I a coward? I think so. On the other hand, maybe God does not want me to do so because this is my last journey of reincarnation and I will be a purple soul after that? If that is true I could blow it by doing this. Maybe I am free after this life? But why do I have to suffer so much in this life? Was I so bad in previous life? At least let me remember that previous bad life so I can enjoy it and be entertained by it. Ha! I am still a bad boy! Sorry.......

The wise man will prefer a state of peace over a state of war! The violent anger is a mental raving; therefore anger is to be avoided for the sake of sanity. But why the sanity? What is wrong with controlled insanity? Fight fire with fire!

Imagine you come home and find that someone has set fire to your house and it has burned to the ground. Your children lay dead in the middle of the floor and you see the killer running away. You immediately try to catch this killer yourself to take action because the police are not interested in doing anything and you are arrested for your actions because they are not in accordance with the law or with the rules of silence. Arrest the first person who creates a disturbance. Whether it is the criminal or the victim is not important. And, after putting the killer through the justice system it is concluded that killer is innocent because he is under age! Impossible? Welcome to western civilization.

Applying the rules of the Old Testament rules and fighting fire with fire would eliminate many of the problems with our justice system. Unfortunately there is no college to teach a parent how to kill the person who was killed their children in the most appropriate way and in the most equal way with the fewest legal consequences. Since the justice system cannot do it right. Shoot the bastard in a middle of the court, drop the gun on a floor and scream that you are the right hand of God and He has directed your actions! You get one year in a mental hospital and after that you are set for a life. You are relieved of the guilt of being a coward and not achieving justice for your children. Congratulations! The reality is that there is no college to teach you quickly how to effectively do this so you wait for the justice system to help. Years pass and you are screwed.

You have two choices. Shoot a bastard in a face, or if he is bigger, go through a back door and shoot him in a back. In a both cases you have the full blessing of God! He fights with evil too. But remember revenge can multiply through members of family, the village country or even the world.

School killings are sad and stupid. But it is not the children's' fault. It is the parents who have created the killing machines. Remember children are born "with no country or religion" as John Lennon sings.

How can parents not know that their children play with guns and explosives in their own garage for years? They have a military training in nearby forests with real guns and finally they order two or three tones of explosives and intend to kill innocent people. Of eighteen people, only three people receive a light sentence and the rest are released home without consequence under the Young Offenders

Act.

These are not children. They are fifteen to twenty-five years old and almost six feet tall. Maybe we should give them each a lollipop before releasing them so they won't cry.

Their brain is like farmers soil. Farmers cultivate soil for years and plant their seeds very carefully.

Who has cultivated these brains and planted these ideas? PARENTS! PARENTS! PARENTS! They should get ten, twenty years or even life sentence for these crimes against society! What happens if these parents send their teenager abroad to military camp to train them to kill our soldiers? He kills them and asks to be taken back as political refugee. No! Is not Mickey Mouse is not Tom and Jerry it is serious. There is a lack of education on how to interpret Commandment #5 in real life.

We have become too civilized and we are unable to kill. All killing is done for us in killing factories; chickens, cows, pigs. They all come to us pre-packaged, already killed. We have lost our basic survivor instinct and ability to kill. So we hope our justice system to do this job for us. But they are the same us. They are unable to kill or isolate a killer for life so we are safe. The killer goes to jail for two years and is free to kill again. So they get three years in jail and are free to kill again, so they get…......See the point? It's a never ending cycle. These killers are behaving according to nature so they are doing their jobs perfectly. We are softened and degenerated by our civilization and we are the one that are not doing our job.

To protect our children from early pregnancy we introduce sex education in schools. To teach them about the food chain we have to educate them on the idea of killing another living animal with no mental reservations or guilt. It is simple; kill that chicken because that is our diner tonight! How do we extend this concept in a way that can protect them from other aspects of life, most importantly....from danger? Can we likewise teach them to kill a killer, or sentence properly that person in court? There is no difference between this chicken and killer. In both cases you have a spiritual obligation to do what is right. Degeneration of our civilization makes us poor killers. We sentence a rapist who rapes torture a child and records this on camera for his enjoyment for, initially, a life sentence and he will be out for good behavior in eight to ten years knowing that there is a possibility that he is going to rape and kill again. And this time he is 100% a predictable machine. It is us who created this problem because we do not know how to kill a chicken.

School should include in the education curriculum subjects like criminology and law with examples of the most severe cases of crimes, and the students should be encouraged to form their own judgments and opinions on the most efficient ways to punish and eliminate the most severe criminals.

Yes, of course; we, ourselves are good and our children are perfect. But somebody said; "there are no thieves, thieves are regular people and could be any one of us." The same is true of children. There are no particular types of children that are bullies or criminals in schools. Any child has the potential to become a bully or criminal. And yes, your child could become one of them. Do not tell me they don't exist because usually you have five bullies per fifty kids. Put your glasses on and take a second look. Perhaps your child is one of those five children. If we all take the time to look carefully perhaps we can make a world for children without bullying and without spreading our adult terroristic ideas in schools. When you put on your imaginary glasses look for that 5% of negativity and not the 95% of amazing beauty that you see every day because your child is a great magician and politician combined and can blind you with one smile. That is all right if your child is not in that negative group but the percentage is extremely high and is in your favor to discover that early because your perfect child can build perfect bombs, or rape or kill. Yes! Each human and child has that potential! The only ingredient you need is a house and ''good parents'. Good parents are the parents who are making more money and spending less time with their children. It starts slowly. First your child becomes a bully or belongs to bully group. And now, they can turn into a sex offender, criminal, drug dealer, political extremist, or worse- become depressed individual driven to suicide or school shootings. Yes that is your little sweetheart. You do not know him or her till you see them in court and the crying parents of the other deceased child.

Yes. I am talking about your child. Each child can turn to this deviation. They are soft. They are like a river which flows easiest way.

Imagine you walk with your child at Halloween dressed as Dracula with big teeth that can bite into somebody neck. The child is maybe five or seven years old. What a horrible thought, right? WRONG! If you do that you are a perfect parent. Imagine what wrong your child can do and you can detect that small percentage of negativeness in them in the future. Your eyes will be open to see the smallest deviation within your child of either being a bully or being the target of a bully. It is not important to go to school and act which can make your child uncomfortable. What is important is to correct your child mentally and use pedagogue to make them love the smaller and weaker people. But, if they are one of the weaker people there is nothing wrong with being a failure and avoiding and running away from the bully.

Nothing to worry about since in the course of their lifetime your child is going to fail many times any way. For the right reasons whether you step away from bullies or fight them is not important as long as you and your child understand situation you are the winners. If your child steps back and the bully repeatedly attack them do not even bother to go to the school. Ask your child to call "Children's Help Line" or "'Children's Bullying Hotline". If not your option is to collect the name of the bully and write a police report at the local police station. Maybe? Is worth it? What does this achieve for yourself or your child? If you achieve something worthwhile for you then that is great. If not, forget it! Step back and use politics and your intelligence to help yourself out of the situation. If you try to talk to the bully's parents and you are not making any progress then go around them and go directly to the police-even if they are friend or neighbors!

Remember, it is difficult to be offended by a barking dog because a dog is far below your intelligence level. If the dog was of equal intelligence it would not bark. But if the dog bites, strike right back at him. That is why it is important to monitor your child's character because that 5% of negativity at 5 years old, instead of 95% goodness can change very quickly to 100% negativity and 0% goodness.

In summary, do not hesitate to punish a criminal because one day the result of this leniency can be unimaginable and can multiply and backfire on society.

COMMANDMENT 6
DO NOT COMMIT ADULTERY

This is a good one. God gave us a sex drive that controls our brain and we should use our brain. But our brain is insane at that moment when you have to make a judgment. It works like this; we have a gland between our legs that controls a gland in our brains. My brain sees a beautiful girl and a gland in my brain sends a hormone signal to gland between my legs, and that gland send a signal back to my brain. So, how much control is left for intelligent decision making?! Fifty percent? A very fragile fifty percent because if she puts her hand on my shoulder or smiles at me this fifty percent will become zero percent control very quickly because the gland that is controlling my judgment is in my brain! I did not make that design, God did!

Lets analyze the entire package of the relationship between men and a women including both love and sex to determinate when adultery occurs and to what degree it has occurred.

I know! Sin is a sin! However, if we don't have some degree of tolerance, and remorse and forgiveness the world will stop existing and that will back fire into our faces. Which means, that people who find themselves on in the wrong path just a little bit will not have the opportunity to redeem themselves and return to the right path. Creating damage to both sides; man and woman.

Let it see how this looks in a little example:

Man and woman fall in love; they build their nest; they build their wealth, and have children. When the man and woman die they cannot take their wealth with them but they can take with them their love and the love they have for their children. They build their karma in this way.

The same man pays a whore one hundred dollars for sex and only money is involved here. No love exists in this relationship. There are no children, there is no nest. In this case no "karma" has been created. Zero achievement, theoretically, but....... (he is happy).

Question? Can his wife satisfy him and stop him from committing adultery? Of course! If she did not have a "headache"! So, as we can see, if "man machine" is over designed with sex, the "woman machine" is often under designed. It takes two to dance....

Everything would be fine if the man's behavior with the whore did not come to light, but God has a sense of humor and He equipped women with a valuable tool known as "women's intuition!" Only God knows what that is. We man find that this instrument that we call "radar" always give us a ticket to pay!!!! Nevertheless; she always finds out where we were! End of the story! What next?

First possibility:

There is a big revolution ending with divorce, alimony, and the suffering of the man, woman and children. Karma is being cut by 50%, 75% or even 100% if depression, alcoholism or even killing occurs!

Second possibility:

There is a small revolution which of course start out bigger, but if remorse kicks in (very important, no yapping, even if they spit in your face!-that is remorse!) things will cool down with time. You would have to overdo yours acts of kindness in the future. But, if yours wife is smart she will have a fewer headaches in the future.... It will be good to both of you, at that moment, to read Commandment #4, of this book of course, to give both of you cold shower.

There is a reason that we say that love is blind. The sex organ that is between the legs does not have eyes and it controls our brain, our decision making and in the end our behavior. We are temporally stupid. But the love have in our marriage is genuine and forever. The love for beautiful chicks was shallow sex, and we love our genuine love, you! Solid love forever and ever. You have to forgive us because God made a mistake when He created people to have imperfections. Two imperfections.......

Signed,
The man.

_____ , (anyone?)
your name here

CHAPTER 6
WHAT IS GOING ON

Yes! We need new commandments! Our world is going insane in much the same way that Moses' world was going insane. We need new rules to make a straight line. The same way that Moses' people were losing control, we are now losing control. This new problem is the alienation of humans.

First we will define a few important terms:

1) Alien; a person from outer space.
2) Alien car driver; a person on a cell phone.
3) Alien husband; a male, occupied by business who sees a child for a few minutes a day and gives the child money in return for love, does routine sex or not, no mental connection to wife, alienation from his wife drifting apart from her. Wife became a stranger= divorce.
4) Industrial alien worker; an office or factory line worker. No heart involved, no brain just hands-on work from nine to five, of course, doctors and lawyers are much more intelligent, so, they have to use their legs during alienation time, to walk from nine to five from patient to patient...
5) Alien politician; a person driven by alien donation toward alien taxes, toward alien military

production, toward alien wars, toward alien killing. Creating alienation of the entire country or even entire world.

Yes! Humans are robots with no awareness of the present they are aliens to themselves. Humans do not have to think about digestion, it happens automatically the same way the heart pumps blood automatically. Internal intelligence runs life inside of humans. Almost 80% of human outside action is similarly controlled automatically. Humans go to work and return home after to watch TV, go to sleep, and go to work, come back....the cycle continues. O! They pup and pee too! Their internal intelligence keeps life running in this circle for them! They do not build their karma they skate through life worthlessly. Awareness is only momentary during child birth, love and death! Only severe pain through the death of a spouse or child death, or terminal sickness creates awareness of being alive. Wake up; look around, what good you can do for others, home, work, city, world, humans or animals?

That is what Jesus tried to show us. His pain and suffering represented His love for us! That is why we measure our love with pain after love one is lost. Tray to measure that when person is alive....

Commandment 7

Do Not Steal

Good one! Steal from whom? This was definitely not God's idea. He thought that everything would be shared equally. Human greediness has created the hell that we are living in.

Today we live in the business mindset of "steal from your friend until he only has the shirt left on his back and then move onto the next friend in line"

This is how life works according to the Old Testament. Big fish eats small fish; the wolf kills the deer; bigger people kill smaller people.

Is the New Testament a set of regulations written by evil in a world where rich people work against good people?

But this was signed by Jesus himself. Was he wrong?

NO! He just did not know the creation of his father and that the world was created to suffer. That is why Jesus was send here to suffer for us. He was unable to correct the creation of his father and he tried to create a democracy in the New Testament but this did not work in practice because the big fish still had to eat the small fish.

He corrected it on paper by trying to introduce the concept of democracy between people but not in a nature. People did not accept this either and continued to kill each other for greed and power. So, what did Jesus achieve?

Guilt for good people who were good before any way or maybe guilt for bad people so that they can become good.

Yes, that's it! That is the beauty of Jesus.

That is the way people think in this sinful world. That is what all nations, cultures and religions today approve;

a) Do not steal from rich people.
b) Do not steal from government.
c) Do not steal from the bank.
d) Do not steal from the clergy.

The only problem is that none of these create any product. They take part of our product, a much larger part, leaving us with a minimal amount which is just enough so that we do not starve and we are still able to produce more for them. And, as if that is not bad enough, they write rules and laws to increase their profit and use police to enforce it!

Let's analyze first what stealing is.

Let's go back to the jungle. Imagine you and your friend chop down trees with an ax to build a shelter. You each chop down two trees a day. But a third man has a gun. He captures ten thousand natives and they in turn chop down for him twenty thousand trees a day. (They don't have shelter either). He comes to you and he sells you trees for half price, but he gives you a mortgage for your house for 10% for rest of your life. Then he forms a government to tax your house a further 10% and further taxes you salary 40%. He creates policemen that can legally shoot you if you refuse to pay or take everything away from you, legally! What will happen if they increase taxes to 100%? Remember they have an army to threaten you with too. Maybe you would try to vote (democratic way) for one of two rich (or representing rich group) candidates which they have already elected behind closed doors. They have brain washed you on TV and have tricked you into believing that you have a say in the outcome when in reality they have already chosen for you. What a democracy!

Now you have a moral right to take back from the rich, what in the beginning belonged to you anyway.

Whatever you steal from him(the third man with a gun) is morally right. He steals from God by taking from others what God gave them to share equally. By breaking God's moral rules he has become a thief. He steals from you. You take back what belong to you. In short, declaring what is considered or not considered stealing is based highly on one's person moral judgment.

If you steal from your friend, neighbor or relative you are a thief.

If you steal from your work (even if you work for the rich) you may lose your job which is a serious consequence. So, you steal from yourself and your family. Ha! Got you! It's a fine line, be careful.

Take back but not from under you. Make a judgment. Did that person make money or use thousand of slaves to work for him?

Now we come to big dilemma:

Normal people have to place to steal. What a pity!

Let me make you instantly rich.

First, I quote you one of the greatest philosopher Locus Seneca (400BC) who said "A cheerful poverty is an honorable state. But if poverty is cheerful then it is not poverty at all. It is not the man who has too little who is poor, but the one who hankers after more!"

So, I ask you; what is maximum wealth for one person before this person is a thief of society?

The answer is simple; first having what is essential and second having what is enough.

This is a personal interpretation which depends on what your starting point was in society. If you were born on a farm and you went to school, became chartered accountant, got married, had a decent salary and enjoyed life with your family (don't forget to look after poor, suffering, and your parents) then you build your "karma" and take it with you to the other side.

However, if you are a chartered accountant all your life and you manipulate money and businesses, you own several factories, cut workers salaries, drive workers to poverty, and kill small businesses then you are a thief.

You have much more than are essential and you

do not stop when you have enough.

You did not spend time with your family or you do not have a family of all (even if you have them they do not know you.) You are not building your "karma" and are therefore wasting your life. You are not taking care of the poor, or those who suffer. Forget about big money for charity. That is smog to kill your conscious with no heart behind the action. Your heart is not behind the factory workers that you throw on a street. You have to come back to repeat your life. You are dead alive now.

If you are born a billionaire and you already own one island, do not buy another one. Why not increase the salary in your factories, improve health care for your workers, open a day care inside a factory and employ single mothers? Why not shift some money to less developed countries? You have what is essential and you have enough. My own private philosophy is; if one cannot create enjoyment for with dollar then one million won't help! Remember God shares equally.

Do not forget to steal!

COMMANDMENT 8
THOU SHALL NOT LIE

You cannot buy consciousness. Your conscience is God in your back conscious brain and it is controlled by your guide, coach or guardian angel. The amount of conscious action is determined by the physical portion of your brain. Remember you have a task to perform on earth in order to build your karma. It is not important that you are going to die. What is important is what you achieve before you die. Your guide can show you the doorway to you goal, but you, physically have to make the decision to walk through it.

The same idea can be seen in the analysis between truth and lies.

Remember a lie repeated a thousand times becomes the truth.

Why? It works two ways. One way is through politics or religion. If you do not agree with their lies they burn you (literally) or shoot you (literally).

The second way is to brainwash you! Whether you are American, Christian, Muslim, Jewish, or German does not matter. You adopt the nationality of the Moon and the religion of Martians, this is all human creation!

Then they can ask you to go and kill in the name of your Moon nationality and Martian God!

The truth always looks like a lie because often seems too simple to be the truth.

So, do not repeat the truth only repeat the lies many, many times so these lies eventually seems to be the truth. After much repetition these lies are burned into your memory so that when you hear them again you say, "O, I remember that!" And you believe it because you can recall these ideas from your own memory. In the end, these lies have become the truth. That how religion and politics work.

Here is an important question. What is a lie?

It is a sin or is a tool to accomplish the truth?

There is no question about it. In the Bible a lie is a sin. But what is a biblical lie? If a three years old boy pees in his pants and say he did not, is he a liar? Yes, but to what degree? Should this be considered a negative lie or positive lie? According to the Catholic Religion, in the fifteen century this boy is a sinner and he should be burned as a punishment. In Cambodia, according to Khmer Rouge Poll Pot Regime this boy should shot in a back of the head. We are humans and such a minor deviation could be judged and punished differently by in times and by different cultures.

So, which lies are considered ordinary lies, and which are considered biblical lies or sins?

First we divide the idea of sins into two categories; sins that are biblical and sins that are harmless politics.

Biblical sins are the one which are connected directly to any of the Commandments. If the Commandment permits you to lie about committing the sin based on the reason that the sin is committed then is it an acceptable political lie. This is where the lies become more political in nature. This is what we can call a political lie and it is considered to be an acceptable lie.

Take for example the commandment "Do not kill". If you do kill and you deny that you did then you lie. But what kind of lie is this? Analyze the situation according to Commandment. If you not permitted to kill and you lie about having killed than this is a Biblical lie and is very straight forward. If you are permitted to kill in a particular situation and you deny that have killed (to save your life in a wrong law system) then this is a Political lie to achieve a truth and justice, where the lie is considered more acceptable. It is as simple as that and each commandment follows the same suit. If a Commandment permits a certain action you can lie about it more acceptably because you are permitted to deviate from the Commandment in the first place. If your action is against a Commandment and you lie about it then you have committed a Biblical lie.

Political lies are permissible ways to achieve the truth, as long as they do not have a wrong or negative intention.

For example, lying to a child can be acceptable in some situations. Telling a child that there is a monster in the basement and not to go down there may be a lie but its intention is to protect the child from entering the dangerous area. In this case there was good and right intentions in telling this lie in order to create goodness. This is a political lie and not a Biblical lie.

Another different example is a government politician promising to lower taxes or to at least keep them the same and he then increases them. This action hurts people and therefore this lie is considered a worse lie because there is wrong intension from the beginning and the outcome is harmful and does not achieve goodness and occurs at the expense of many people. This lie is a Biblical lie.

In conclusion there are two different kinds of lies. In order to judge whether a lie should be considered a Biblical lie or a Political lie you must analyze them against the basic Commandments and take into consideration the initial intension of the lie and the outcome created by the lie itself.

BUT IF POLITICS IS BAD, IT IS A LIE!

P.S. Ha! Now you confuse completely…that is good, that is intension of this book, to make you thinking…

COMMANDMENT 11

LIFE AND DEATH

When we come close to the end of our lives, we must synchronize human life with our sole purpose for being here and try to put these into alignment. There is no difference between death and birth. It is the same transformation but in the reverse order. Death is a happy moment because your soul friends who were very sad when you left them to be born into physical life are welcoming you back to the spiritual world.

This is the same transformation that occurs during one's birth at which time you were transferred from the spiritual world to the physical world and your soul was injected into a human body. With your birth your earth family is happy and your spiritual family is sad at your having left the spiritual world. In death your earth family is sad and your soul family is happy that you have been reborn through death. Let's see if there are any similarities or references to our dying body and soul during life.

Souls after death exist in the form of lights. It is interesting to see if colored auras are emitted by the human body during a life and photographed by Kirlian photography has any relationship with colors of souls after death? We know that aura around the human body reflects thoughts, emotions, feelings and health information and that was reflected in Kirlian's photography. How much can be learned by studying the phenomena of colors and body aura from a living being for the purpose of studying human beings physically and spiritually and how can we use this medically to improve human life?

According to hypnosis by Dr .Michael Newton the color of soul light depends on how advance the soul is according to how many times soul has come back to earth and how old and experienced the soul is. But, human light reflected under Kirlian photography is light from a living soul. Are there any similarities between these two or not?

Dr. Newton, who obtained information from hypnotized patients by putting them back into a time before they were born reports that souls are divided into groups. The first group is categorized as Young Souls, who are first time on earth. These souls have a white bright color of light. A second category are categorized as More Mature Souls with yellowish color going slowly to blue. The final category is categorized as Masters Souls which are dark blue and go to the highest color of purple. According to people who were hypnotized and were between lives (between death and next life), each soul is placed into a cluster of souls that they know from earth. They study mistakes from previous lives so they can mature and correct these errors in their next life. Their coaches (guardian angels, who became their life's conscience throughout their life) coach them to correct their mistakes and choose their new life not only for happiness but also for suffering for the mistakes they have made in their previous life or lives.

In some very bad cases souls are displaced due to criminal abnormalities in human body. Spiritual guides deliberately remove them from association with other souls for indeterminate periods of time for the purpose of rehabilitation and these souls are coached separately. Each soul has a personal guide. Some people who meditate can come to a state of enlightenment and are able to to see or contact their personal guides. This often happens to people who are unconscious or children up to four years old. That is why many children want to have a light on overnight because they are confused between reality and their guardian who still visits them and are often referred to as an imaginary friend. Their memory of this slowly diminishes. They tell people about their personal friend that visits them in their room but of course adults do not believe them.

We adults are receiving information from our guardians through pure conscience but they don't force us, they just suggest.....

Each soul has different character and integrity. Integrity is the desire to be honest about self motivation and to find a path to the "fullness's of goodness". Progression of souls and difficulties of life mature them much faster into awareness of perfection so they don't have to come back here anymore. These souls become purple. Now stop for a moment! Look around, how much "fullness of goodness" do you see? NONE! There are only ugly humans creating wars and killing entire villages with families so they can expand their imperialistic greedy markets. YES, YOU! You want a bigger car, you want a bigger house, and because you not see it doesn't mean you are not involved! There is blood on your extravagant toys, you just put your head in the sand and ignore it and you watch things that are happening in the news like from Disneyland. If you eat Kentucky Fried Chicken you kill a chicken. Fine, we did not create this world we do not know why we have to do that but if we pay a soldier to kill innocent people across the globe so we can have more oil for bigger cars we become "PROFESSIONAL KILLERS WITH CLEAN HANDS" WITH OUR HEADS IN THE SAND SO WE CAN PRETEND THAT WE DO NOT SEE OUR INVOLVMENT.

You could be a weak soul, collecting money for your charity, or strong soul like a soldier abroad carving your life in a manner right or wrong. The worst kind of humans are free skaters, salesman, bankers, politicians, people living well, without any connection to either end of this spectrum. That is our amplitude from collecting to killing!

So people whose children are fighting abroad who have not been killed yet still have to wake up. It is the only way that they will understand the severity of the situation because they are directly affected by it. Is the only way that people will understand the gravity of the situation is if they lose their own children? The answer unfortunately is yes.

The result to ignorance to the real situation has created problems including 9-11 and the collapse of Chrysler or GM. That is price of ignorance. We are a part of the universe; every part of our body is a little universe with electrons circulating around atom centers. We are synchronized with the entire universe and we vibrate with the right frequency so we can become one with the universe.

All three souls, collecting money for charity, fighting abroad, or skating through life, can have similar difficulties for building their awareness and love (karma) so they can step up the ladder from an ordinary white soul to a more yellow soul.

As we learn from the people that were hypnotize and put back to a previous life, this knowledge must come through self discovery. Even as victims we are beneficiaries because it is how we stand up to failure and duress which really marks our progress in life.

Most interesting is that during hypnosis is possible to question adults about times when they were still a child. Children are honest and they cannot lie! Ha! Ha! They cannot lie? Is that not fun? We can ask them embarrassing questions......

But not everything is fun. Our family is very often dishonest, greedy, ugly and selfish. They could be possessive sadistic and cruel. Through our suffering and their mistakes we can develop our souls to better understanding and step up our soul's development into a higher level so we can glow in higher colors.

It is karmic purpose to receive pain or pleasure from someone close to us. Remember we not only come to learn our lessons but we also play a part in others' life lessons. Sometimes a soul can become bossy to a physical body on earth. In these cases the 50% balance between the physical freedom and spiritual task assignment is forgotten. At that moment spiritual unbalance can came to religious fanatics as physical unbalance can create degeneration that can lead to criminal, sexual and cruel behavior. It is up to us to take a deep breath, ask our conscious how to correct ourselves and start again. If not we have to come back in a next life to suffer for this behavior. So, what is the sense of doing that? It is like grabbing a hammer and hitting yourself in the finger. Why not stopping the hammer half way and avoid the pain and look for ways to create pleasure? Ha! That is impossible! We are humans! We have to create pain and suffering because we are stupid. This is the weakness of human beings.

These cruel souls require special coaching, separate from others, they are going to receive extra difficult assignments to overcome and they have to climb from negative to zero point even before they can begin to climb the ladder of goodness.

If yours soul is confused about its own life and does not know where to turn to next, just relax, close your eyes and sleep on it. Most of the time your guide, through your conscience will direct you and the answer will come to you.

Dr. Michael Newton covers very nicely the middle section but he is scared to death to go any further. He covers "blue workers", people's souls, and higher levels of coaches all the way to the eternity of purple soul. Beautiful, but he does not go above that to touch on the subject of elders or The Mighty One, meaning God. And this is the different between people who only study these experiences as opposed to those who have lived through such an experience.

I lived through such an experience. And that what inspired me to write this book. My deceased seventeen year old daughter was talking to me and I was so stupid, so stupid that I could not believe it! I am technically educated. How could I believe it? She was telling me about the color of flowers on other side and how beautiful they were. That is what she was telling me. Am I stupid or what? She was telling me how beautiful it is on another side while I was repairing sophisticated electronic equipment and trying to earn a living. How could I believe it? Growing up She did not allow us to shut the light off in her bedroom when she went to sleep because, she reported that when the light was off elderly people came to her and discussed different events and tasks for her. They also told her that she was clear and she could leave at any time she wanted! So, do you think this was a child's imagination? Let's go to the facts! Born on December 25th-Jesus' birthday. Coincidence? I did not believe her the 10 or 20 times she reported these strange visits to me. I did not believe her the 30 or 40 times she reported them to me. What is the limit? When does it become possible to believe something that is unbelievable? Wait and see it.! At the age of three she could ski, at four she could read at a level of five to eight year olds. In school teachers wanted to remove her from classes because she was so distracted and they thought she was mentally unfit because she was drawing teacher and student portraits with adult quality and perfection. Or she would stay outside in a school yard catching worms or butterflies and studying them with magnifying glass. Fortunately there was nothing teachers could do because she always achieved 100% academic results in 5% time compared with rest of the students in her classes. And, she walked away in a middle of the exam to find her worms and butterflies despite her angry teachers. She simply declared that the programs are too childish and she was bored so she started concentrating on arts, sports and charity ignoring all teachers and school authorities! At the age of 12 she was the Ontario Junior Moguls Ski Champion. She had natural talents. With no formal training in sport or art, she just did everything perfectly -scary. Ontario ski race champion, age 15 senior GS Ontario Snowboard Champion, focused on making the Nagano Olympic Team at Age 16, best Brampton painter artist in oil, pencil and water painting. Three awards in photography. And, big headache to me, many single parent girl friends that slept over in my house for weeks at a time that I was happy to feed, take to my cottage, teach skiing, and take on ski vacations. She always said that she had to pay back to society for her successes by helping to others. Oh well I loved and enjoy them very much.

We both work as ski-snowboard instructors in Hockley Valley Resort. When my daughter became 16 they fired us, proclaiming that two members of the same family cannot work at the same resort. I wrote an article in the newspaper that this is racism and they kicked us out after 10 years of excellent, professional, personal and family relationships with management and owners. She stood in the middle of the ski hill, crying, she said; only humans can do that. It was very sad.

And now, that is first kicker, we went to Mansfield Club to get new ski-snowboarding job .They called us up in front of four members of the management team and she whispered into my ear, daddy this persons is bad, bad, bad. And she point to three out of four of the interviewers. I asked how you know?! And she answer, daddy I told you that I can see through people and I can see other side but you never listen or believed, you are too technical! A few years later I found out from a friend that she was right. After she died, Hockley Valley Resorts call me and offered me a Snowboard Supervisor Position which I accepted for a few years to show them that I forgave them, but did not approve them. But were they intelligent enough to read that? How much of that was remorse and how much of it was direction from my daughter from above is a mystery.

These examples are nothing, nothing, compared with being touched directly from other side.

Two years after my daughter's death I crossed the border from Canada to New York State to buy a gun.

Everybody knows that guns in US you can eat for breakfast, but not in NY! Gun laws are very strict in New York State. I did not know that. I was suicidal, and completely delusional. I could have jumped in front of a train or into highway traffic. Nevertheless, I entered a gun shop- a legal gun shop with no illegal intentions. I ask for a gun. They refused me immediately, but they give me a telephone number to call and they told me that there would be no problem but I would have to buy it privately.

I called the number and the man on the other end if the line said he would meet me in one hour at McDonalds. I needed to waste some time before meeting this person so I drove into a residential street, I open a car door, got out and leaned on the driver's side of the car and I heard; "DADDY DON'T DO IT!"

I looked left, I looked right, and there was nobody there! Feeling? It was the same way that she told me about color of the flowers on another side! I am intelligent man, nobody! Nobody, can tell me about the color of the flowers on the other side! And I heard her again this time so loud that if I had volume control I would decrease it because it was so painful. "DADDY DON'TDO IT!" Tears started pouring from my eyes. I looked left and I looked right. Still nobody. So I answered "Yvonne, I know, I know!, I hear you! Where are you? I want to see you!"

And now I was standing fully alert with full awareness prepared to observe the unbelievable.

I was looking left and right with both hands on the roof of my car. I was prepared for disbelief, and it came. "DADDY DON'T DO IT!" So loud! But directly to my brain. I don't think anybody else could hear it. Nevertheless I answered, "I know they going to get me but that is only way I can show you how much I love you."

That is the reason that I decided to write this book. So there will be no chapter titled "Vision" as I planned in my introduction. It came suddenly into this chapter.

I met the fellow at McDonalds where he insisted I buy two guns minimum. Although I did not want two guns I did buy two guns and I left. On the way to my car I saw a garbage can. I had the temptation to throw the package into the garbage. I felt that the message from my daughter above was a warning to me that this was a set-up and that by throwing the guns away I could avoid legal consequences. But I did not use the information that I had been given because I still felt that following through with my plan was the only way I could show Yvonne how much I loved her.

Maybe that is why Jesus suffered on the cross to show us how much He loves us. Maximum pain for maximum love.

Nevertheless five minutes after I left McDonald's I had five police cars surround me. I could have thrown the package in garbage but I did not. I wanted to suffer for Yvonne, for maximum love!

The police charged me with gun distributing which is why the undercover officer insisted on me buying two guns. Yes! That is right. In short, the police sold guns on the street to a mentally unstable grieving parent who lost his only child so that they could charge him with gun smuggling. What would have happened if I committed suicide? That's too bad... What would have happen if I start shooting other people? Who make such a decision?

What a beautiful piece of police work. None of the officers involved in my arrest showed up in a court when they discovered my situation. I had a Lawyer, a beautiful Jewish woman, a mother of two children, to defend me in court. We cried together many times. In court all my friends cried, the defense cried, and the judge cried. The police were too ashamed to show their faces in court.

After hearing "DADDY DON'T DO IT" so clearly, can I say I was touched by an Angel? And, does this give me the right to write this book? I think it does.

If above story is definitely "life and death" story, let's go back to our new commandment, Life and Death, to progress in chronological order.

Now let's touch on the topic of re-birth. So happy birthday to you. You die happily and your soul's relatives are happy and they sing happy birthday to you when you return to the spiritual world. What next? First look at where you are on the topic of death. At the beginning of this book you were scared to death to die and now you are happy to die. Well, maybe not exactly happy but is getting better is it not? During death you meet your coach, your conscience, your Guardian Angel. Finally you can punch him in the face. "Why was I not rich, strong, and smart? You son of a gun?" We can beat him up now for our failures. It is not so. We build our karma our self, we create our failures. Your coach can only advise you. In the end we can only punch ourselves in the face for our failures. Our next step is to analyze our previous life and according to that we will choose what our next life will be and how we will pay for our mistakes or what rewards we will take for our successes. However, we still have to come back to earth until our soul becomes the color purple in order to be free. This theory is presented in Dr. Newton's book **The Journey of Souls.** And his information is gathered from hypnotized patients who seem to be reliable and believable.

According to these hypnotized patients during rebirth they come down to Earth through the same tunnel, similar to a death tunnel, but more silky and smooth, until they land inside a mother's baby.

Now, we know that before re-birth these souls went to classes of self improvements and analyzed previous life mistakes and success. They were coached on how to improve and correct their previous life and how to plan their next one in a way that will correct and improve their karma to a higher soul level. The coach will release us to new life with new tasks and coach us through the first year or two and later becomes our conscious mind. We enter a baby inside a mother's womb and life commences physically and spiritually.

Throughout the birth process we have amnesia regarding our previous life. We remain attached to our coach through the first few years. However, we are not ever abandoned even if the developing baby is of lower intelligence or soul maturity in the beginning. The soul is bonded with the body for life regardless of whether it is of lower or higher intelligence, or experiencing pain or pleasure so we can learn lessons and achieve higher awareness. Otherwise the soul can leave the body during pain and come back during pleasure. In early stages of development then there are lower levels of intelligence in the baby the soul tries to develop the baby's character away from previous life mistakes. And that is essential for creating the new direction in life that was carefully planned in the coach's classes to build karma and higher awareness.

In my opinion the soul has complete amnesia throughout the birth process as does the body. Both the soul and the body regain full spiritual awareness through death and the only attachment to the original task that we came here to perform is our conscious mind but we approve the action with our physical power. What is mysterious in this process is how returned souls can have a higher or lower level tasks on Earth. Are there different levels of coaches or spiritual advisors that prepare various souls for different levels? Why are we not meeting higher level of advisors during hypnosis?

The more I write this book the more I like a people. And, hopefully the more you read this book the less you fear death.

The people that passing me, they all smile, because I see theirs karma, not their present action.

Nevertheless the beauty of this book is that we are writing, talking about and discussing this subject and each of us brings one brick at a time to build an understanding of the world of spiritualism. We open a door to God as Religion closes this subject in a capsule of time. No more storks bringing babies. No more Santa Claus for adults.

Chapter 11
Present Life and Death

This chapter will deal with new interpretation of each Commandment in our present modern life.

This chapter will also admit that we are fully trained to accept responsibility for our own deaths and also to be responsible for living fulfilling lives according to moral rules of nature and not rules imposed by man. Remember if you follow nature you will never be poor, and if you follow people you will never be rich. Let us see how people react in cases of crisis.

People who are near death often cry because they are going to die. But, if you tell them that one thousand years from now they are not going to be alive and that one thousand years ago they were not alive it does not bother them. Why? Because one thousand years ago these people were not attached with love to relatives, shiny cars, or beautiful houses. What this means is that they do not want to leave the present beauty and possessions and go to the unknown. How often do we complete daily routines over and over again, never changing. It is almost like we are already dead but living, waiting for an end; an end that we are afraid of.

And that is what this book is going to help you

understand. From this point on you are going to practice during your life how to die and how to live.

Very often we are so alienated from life that it is almost as if we are dead. Let's open our eyes and analyze a few situations from our lives

Homeless people, for example windshield cleaners, are constantly asking for change. "Do you have a dollar, or even twenty five cents"? Why not go crazy and give them ten or twenty dollars?. Temporarily you will be broke but look in the rear view mirror and see that smile! Yes! That is your face! And you say "I am a crazy son of a gun, so why I have that big smile on my face"? The answer is simple. It is that there are no angels they are only Angels' Acts completed by humans. What you did is an Angel Act and you have an Angel's smile on your face. When you take a shower tonight look for some feathers on your back…

Another example from life is one's Spouse. It is so easy to get angry or even violent toward your spouse; mostly the man toward the woman._ But how offend today in the western world anger is turned towards a loving man, man that is to shame to loudly complain...

This is an easy problem to correct. For example: A man, who has lost his job, has high mortgage, a single income family and three kids comes home shaking, ready to cry. He does not know how to explain to his wife that the family may suffer due to their financial situation and that they might end up with no house or food.

Stalling for time and courage he first makes a cup of coffee, stirring it slowly with a spoon and then put the spoon gently on the counter. Finally he says "Honey, I lost my job", she looks at him and screams;

"I HAVE BEEN CLEANING ALL DAY AND YOU PUT A SPOON ON THE COUNTER? GET OUT OF "MY"HOUSE!"

And she is right. A woman's world is different than a man's world. She has a nest with young one, and she will bite anyone, even her own man, if he gets too close and becomes a danger. At that moment no man in the world is allowed to use any physical force against that beautiful (but emotional) creature-woman. Even if she jumps on you, what is that? A mosquito bite? If you are a real man with muscles, you think to hug her when she hits you but you never even think to touch her!

The woman is weaker so it is no physical achievement for the man who beats her at something. It is like wining a boxing match against a small child and boasting to a grown man "I won! See how strong I am." What you are really saying is "look at what a terrible person I am." Winning an unfair fight with a weaker person is always a failure. She is female and she will take care of the your babies weather you alive or not. What is wrong with this situation? They did not practice their love from a life and death perspective. Their love is shallow and can be blown away in the wind. Let see how a person who has read this book can find the correct

answer for the above situation.
You do not know what you have till you lose it.

1. They fall in love. If one of them dies, how much do they value theirs loss?
2. They buy a house. If they lose that house (death of the house) what is emotional loss from that?
3. First child is born. What happens if the mother or the child dies? How valuable is that loss?
4. Second child is born. What happens if the mother or the child dies? Is this the same loss?
5. Third child is born. What happens if the mother or the child dies?
6. The coffee spoon on the counter- is that more important than all of the above questions? That is what she is thinking at that moment. That is what she wants.

Is this a joke? No, it is life. Let us see what she would do if she could meditate according to "Life and Death" in this book.

Her thought process:
I love my husband. I do not want him to die.
I love my children. I do not want them to die.
I love my house. I do not want it to lose it.
I do not love a coffee spoon…ha ha, now she can see how funny this is.

What if she thinks about the possibility that her husband and three children could die and that they could lose their house? Suddenly this thought seems horrible and the thought of her husband only losing his job is not so bad and she jumps and hugs him. Because she knows what greater things she can lose and knows how to value the real important things in life. The important thing in life it not that we die, this is inevitable, it is what we do before we die that matters.

Another example are teenagers. Teenagers are like space ships coming back to earth. They lose communication with base for a while but if they are built well they come back. If parents did their job well during childhood the children will not do anything wrong during the "black out" period and they come back with full love. During the "black out" period parents pick up the fruit of the seeds they have planted inside their children. Do not tale me that when farmer plant an onion seed a rose may grow! If 18 teenagers collected several tones of explosives to blow up innocent working people, do not tell me that their parents sent them to ski clubs. Parents should get a life sentence in prison for the actions of these children. If you are intelligent you will understand what I am talking about.

After one year of university authorities catch your child smoking "pot". He or She finishes university and becomes successful in life. This is mild growing pains. There is nothing wrong with experimenting with a little bit of wrong to learn what is right. These teenagers come back to base after the black out period.

Why did the first group of 18 teenagers express their hate and express themselves through violence? Because theirs space ship was build inside a dark box and they never were able to think outside of the box. They did not receive love from parents and they do not see that they are loved. They did not realize that they had to build their karma the same as everyone else. The only thing that they have to do is to open their arms towards us. Ours are open already.

The final example is Elderly people. They are like children again often with limited intelligent and in diapers. So, why is it so cute to change a diaper on a child and so unpleasant on an elderly person? The answer is simple. It is the same as sex organs of a loved partner being so beautiful, but the sex organs of the elderly not so. They are the same except that the sex gland which control our brains make us temporally blind, so we think our partner is so beautiful and elderly are not. It is only our state of mind. How we can correct that? With love and pleasant memories from the life lived with this person. Important memories such as special events like guiding us trough elementary school or high school, birthdays, gifts and things that were sacrificed for us. Now take these memories and thoughts in one package and change that diaper. With time you get used to it although men do not like to change diaper on babies ether....

The purpose of this book is to bring an awareness to people so that they can evolve to conscious beings that have come to this world with a specific task to perform and to not fall into a daily routine of living that causes you to drift into a life of alienation. Those who do not wake up will suffer the consequences of their unconsciousness.

Amazon
tradth of live
2014